SET-1

1. Hello World:

```java
public class HelloWorld {
    public static void main(String[] args) {
        System.out.println("Hello, World!");
    }
}
```

2. Add Two Numbers:

```java
public class AddTwoNumbers {
    public static void main(String[] args) {
        int num1 = 5, num2 = 15, sum;
        sum = num1 + num2;
        System.out.println("Sum of these numbers: " + sum);
    }
}
```

3. Factorial of a Number:

```java
public class Factorial {
    public static void main(String[] args) {
        int num = 5;
        long factorial = 1;
        for (int i = 1; i <= num; ++i) {
            factorial *= i;
        }
        System.out.println("Factorial of " + num + " = " + factorial);
    }
}
```

4. Fibonacci Series:

```java
public class Fibonacci {
    public static void main(String[] args) {
        int n = 10, t1 = 0, t2 = 1;
        System.out.print("Fibonacci Series: ");
        for (int i = 1; i <= n; ++i) {
            System.out.print(t1 + " + ");
            int sum = t1 + t2;
            t1 = t2;
            t2 = sum;
        }
    }
}
```

5. Reverse a String:

```java
public class ReverseString {
    public static void main(String[] args) {
        String str = "Hello World";
        String reversed = new StringBuilder(str).reverse().toString();
        System.out.println("Reversed string: " + reversed);
    }
}
```

6. Check for Even or Odd:

```java
public class EvenOrOdd {
    public static void main(String[] args) {
        int num = 5;
        if (num % 2 == 0) {
            System.out.println("The number is even.");
        } else {
            System.out.println("The number is odd.");
        }
    }
}
```

7. Check for Prime Number:

```java
public class PrimeNumber {
    public static void main(String[] args) {
        int num = 29;
        boolean flag = false;
        for (int i = 2; i <= num / 2; ++i) {
            if (num % i == 0) {
                flag = true;
                break;
            }
        }
        if (!flag)
            System.out.println(num + " is a prime number.");
        else
            System.out.println(num + " is not a prime number.");
    }
}
```

8. Sum of Natural Numbers:

```java
public class SumOfNaturalNumbers {
    public static void main(String[] args) {
        int num = 10, sum = 0;
```

```java
        for (int i = 1; i <= num; ++i) {

            sum += i;

        }

        System.out.println("Sum = " + sum);

    }

}
```

9. Generate Multiplication Table:

```java
public class MultiplicationTable {

    public static void main(String[] args) {

        int num = 5;

        for (int i = 1; i <= 10; ++i) {

            System.out.printf("%d * %d = %d \n", num, i, num * i);

        }

    }

}
```

10. Find Largest Among Three Numbers:

```java
public class LargestAmongThree {

    public static void main(String[] args) {

        double n1 = 5, n2 = 7, n3 = 3;

        if (n1 >= n2 && n1 >= n3)
```

```java
        System.out.println(n1 + " is the largest number.");
    else if (n2 >= n1 && n2 >= n3)
        System.out.println(n2 + " is the largest number.");
    else
        System.out.println(n3 + " is the largest number.");
    }
}
```

SET-2

1. Find the Maximum Element in an Array:

```java
public class MaxElement {
    public static void main(String[] args) {
        int[] arr = { 1, 4, 7, 2, 9, 3 };
        int max = arr[0];
        for (int i = 1; i < arr.length; i++) {
            if (arr[i] > max) {
                max = arr[i];
            }
        }
        System.out.println("Maximum element in the array: " + max);
    }
}
```

2. Calculate Average of Array Elements:

```java
public class AverageArray {
    public static void main(String[] args) {
        double[] numbers = { 2.5, 3.4, 1.9, 4.3, 3.2 };
        double sum = 0.0;
        for (double num : numbers) {
            sum += num;
        }
        double average = sum / numbers.length;
        System.out.println("Average value of the array elements is : " + average);
    }
}
```

3. Check if a String is a Palindrome:

```java
public class PalindromeCheck {
    public static void main(String[] args) {
        String original = "madam";
        String reverse = "";
        for (int i = original.length() - 1; i >= 0; i--) {
            reverse = reverse + original.charAt(i);
        }
        if (original.equals(reverse)) {
```

```java
            System.out.println("The string is a palindrome.");
        } else {
            System.out.println("The string is not a palindrome.");
        }
    }
}
```

4. Calculate Factorial using Recursion:

```java
public class FactorialRecursive {
    public static void main(String[] args) {
        int num = 5;
        long factorial = multiplyNumbers(num);
        System.out.println("Factorial of " + num + " = " + factorial);
    }
    public static long multiplyNumbers(int num) {
        if (num >= 1)
            return num * multiplyNumbers(num - 1);
        else
            return 1;
    }
}
```

5. Display Characters of a String:

```java
public class DisplayCharacters {
    public static void main(String[] args) {
        String str = "Hello";
        for (int i = 0; i < str.length(); i++) {
            System.out.print(str.charAt(i) + " ");
        }
    }
}
```

6. Swap Two Numbers:

```java
public class SwapNumbers {
    public static void main(String[] args) {
        float first = 1.20f, second = 2.45f;
        System.out.println("--Before swap--");
        System.out.println("First number: " + first);
        System.out.println("Second number: " + second);
        // Value swap
        float temporary = first;
        first = second;
        second = temporary;
        System.out.println("--After swap--");
        System.out.println("First number: " + first);
        System.out.println("Second number: " + second);
```

```
  }
}
```

7. Calculate Power of a Number:

```java
public class PowerOfNumber {
    public static void main(String[] args) {
        int base = 3, exponent = 4;
        long result = 1;
        while (exponent != 0) {
            result *= base;
            --exponent;
        }
        System.out.println("Answer = " + result);
    }
}
```

8. Print ASCII Value of a Character:

```java
public class ASCIIValue {
    public static void main(String[] args) {
        char ch = 'a';
        int ascii = ch;
        System.out.println("The ASCII value of " + ch + " is: " + ascii);
```

```
        }
}
```

9. Display Prime Numbers between Two Intervals:

```java
public class PrimeIntervals {
    public static void main(String[] args) {
        int low = 20, high = 50;
        while (low < high) {
            boolean flag = false;
            for (int i = 2; i <= low / 2; ++i) {
                if (low % i == 0) {
                    flag = true;
                    break;
                }
            }
            if (!flag)
                System.out.print(low + " ");
            ++low;
        }
    }
}
```

10. Find the GCD (Greatest Common Divisor) of Two Numbers:

```java
public class GCD {
    public static void main(String[] args) {
        int n1 = 81, n2 = 153;
        while (n1 != n2) {
            if (n1 > n2)
                n1 -= n2;
            else
                n2 -= n1;
        }
        System.out.println("G.C.D = " + n1);
    }
}
```

SET-3

1. Check Leap Year:

```java
public class LeapYear {
    public static void main(String[] args) {
        int year = 2024;
        boolean leap = false;
        if (year % 4 == 0) {
            if (year % 100 == 0) {
                if (year % 400 == 0)
```

```java
                leap = true;
            else
                leap = false;
        } else
            leap = true;
    } else
        leap = false;
    if (leap)
        System.out.println(year + " is a leap year.");
    else
        System.out.println(year + " is not a leap year.");
    }
}
```

2. Reverse an Array:

```java
import java.util.Arrays;

public class ReverseArray {
    public static void main(String[] args) {
        int[] array = { 1, 2, 3, 4, 5 };
        System.out.println("Original Array: " + Arrays.toString(array));
        for (int i = 0; i < array.length / 2; i++) {
            int temp = array[i];
            array[i] = array[array.length - 1 - i];
```

```java
            array[array.length - 1 - i] = temp;
        }
        System.out.println("Reversed Array: " + Arrays.toString(array));
    }
}
```

3. Count the Number of Words in a String:

```java
public class CountWords {
    public static void main(String[] args) {
        String str = "This is a sample sentence.";
        int count = 1;
        for (int i = 0; i < str.length(); i++) {
            if (str.charAt(i) == ' ' && str.charAt(i + 1) != ' ') {
                count++;
            }
        }
        System.out.println("Number of words in the string: " + count);
    }
}
```

4. Calculate Simple Interest:

```java
public class SimpleInterest {
```

```java
    public static void main(String[] args) {

        double principle = 2000;

        double rate = 3;

        double time = 1.5;

        double simpleInterest = (principle * time * rate) / 100;

        System.out.println("Simple Interest is: " + simpleInterest);

    }

}
```

5. Check if a Number is a Perfect Number:

```java
public class PerfectNumber {

    public static void main(String[] args) {

        int num = 28;

        int sum = 0;

        for (int i = 1; i < num; i++) {

            if (num % i == 0) {

                sum += i;

            }

        }

        if (sum == num) {

            System.out.println(num + " is a perfect number.");

        } else {

            System.out.println(num + " is not a perfect number.");

        }
```

```
        }
}
```

6. Check for Armstrong Number:

```java
public class ArmstrongNumber {
    public static void main(String[] args) {
        int number = 371, originalNumber, remainder, result = 0;
        originalNumber = number;
        while (originalNumber != 0) {
            remainder = originalNumber % 10;
            result += Math.pow(remainder, 3);
            originalNumber /= 10;
        }
        if (result == number)
            System.out.println(number + " is an Armstrong number.");
        else
            System.out.println(number + " is not an Armstrong number.");
    }
}
```

7. Sort Elements in an Array:

```java
import java.util.Arrays;
```

```java
public class ArraySort {
    public static void main(String[] args) {
        int[] arr = { 13, 7, 6, 45, 21, 9, 101, 102 };
        Arrays.sort(arr);
        System.out.println("Sorted Array: " + Arrays.toString(arr));
    }
}
```

8. Find the LCM (Least Common Multiple) of Two Numbers:

```java
public class LCM {
    public static void main(String[] args) {
        int n1 = 72, n2 = 120, lcm;
        lcm = (n1 > n2) ? n1 : n2;
        while (true) {
            if (lcm % n1 == 0 && lcm % n2 == 0) {
                System.out.printf("The LCM of %d and %d is %d.", n1, n2, lcm);
                break;
            }
            ++lcm;
        }
    }
}
```

9. Remove White Spaces from a String:

```java
public class RemoveWhiteSpaces {
    public static void main(String[] args) {
        String str = "  Hello  World  ";
        str = str.replaceAll("\\s", "");
        System.out.println("String after removing white spaces: " + str);
    }
}
```

10. Find the Frequency of Characters in a String:

```java
import java.util.HashMap;

public class CharacterFrequency {
    public static void main(String[] args) {
        String str = "hello world";
        HashMap<Character, Integer> map = new HashMap<>();
        for (char c : str.toCharArray()) {
            if (map.containsKey(c)) {
                map.put(c, map.get(c) + 1);
            } else {
                map.put(c, 1);
            }
```

```
        }
        System.out.println("Character frequency in the string: " + map);
    }
}
```

SET-4

1. Calculate the Area of a Circle:

```
public class AreaOfCircle {
    public static void main(String[] args) {
        double radius = 3;
        double area = Math.PI * radius * radius;
        System.out.println("Area of the circle is: " + area);
    }
}
```

2. Create and Use a Class:

```
class Rectangle {
    int length;
    int width;

    public int calculateArea() {
```

```java
        return length * width;
    }
}


public class UseRectangle {
    public static void main(String[] args) {
        Rectangle rect = new Rectangle();
        rect.length = 5;
        rect.width = 3;
        int area = rect.calculateArea();
        System.out.println("Area of the rectangle is: " + area);
    }
}
```

3. Implement Inheritance:

```java
class Vehicle {
    void display() {
        System.out.println("This is a vehicle.");
    }
}


class Car extends Vehicle {
    void displayCar() {
        System.out.println("This is a car.");
```

```
        }
}


public class InheritanceExample {

    public static void main(String[] args) {

        Car car = new Car();

        car.display();

        car.displayCar();

    }

}
```

4. Calculate the Power of a Number using Math.pow():

```
public class PowerExample {

    public static void main(String[] args) {

        double base = 2, exponent = 3;

        double result = Math.pow(base, exponent);

        System.out.println("Result: " + result);

    }

}
```

5. Create a Simple Calculator using Methods:

```
public class Calculator {
```

```java
    public static void main(String[] args) {
        System.out.println("Addition: " + add(5, 3));
        System.out.println("Subtraction: " + subtract(5, 3));
        System.out.println("Multiplication: " + multiply(5, 3));
        System.out.println("Division: " + divide(5, 3));
    }

    public static int add(int a, int b) {
        return a + b;
    }

    public static int subtract(int a, int b) {
        return a - b;
    }

    public static int multiply(int a, int b) {
        return a * b;
    }

    public static double divide(int a, int b) {
        return (double) a / b;
    }
}
```

6. Use of Constructor in Java:

```java
class Student {
    String name;
    int age;

    Student(String name, int age) {
        this.name = name;
        this.age = age;
    }

    void display() {
        System.out.println("Name: " + name + " Age: " + age);
    }
}

public class ConstructorExample {
    public static void main(String[] args) {
        Student student = new Student("John", 20);
        student.display();
    }
}
```

7. Implement Interface in Java:

```java
interface Shape {
```

```java
    void draw();
}

class Circle implements Shape {
    public void draw() {
        System.out.println("Drawing Circle");
    }
}

public class InterfaceExample {
    public static void main(String[] args) {
        Circle circle = new Circle();
        circle.draw();
    }
}
```

8. Use of Encapsulation in Java:

```java
class Encapsulate {
    private String name;
    private int age;

    public String getName() {
        return name;
    }
}
```

```java
    public void setName(String name) {

        this.name = name;

    }


    public int getAge() {

        return age;

    }


    public void setAge(int age) {

        this.age = age;

    }

}


public class EncapsulationExample {

    public static void main(String[] args) {

        Encapsulate obj = new Encapsulate();

        obj.setName("John");

        obj.setAge(20);

        System.out.println("Name: " + obj.getName());

        System.out.println("Age: " + obj.getAge());

    }

}
```

9. Use of Static Keyword in Java:

```java
class Counter {
    static int count = 0;

    Counter() {
        count++;
        System.out.println(count);
    }
}

public class StaticExample {
    public static void main(String[] args) {
        Counter c1 = new Counter();
        Counter c2 = new Counter();
        Counter c3 = new Counter();
    }
}
```

10. Exception Handling in Java:

```java
public class ExceptionExample {
    public static void main(String[] args) {
        try {
            int[] arr = { 1, 2, 3, 4, 5 };
            System.out.println(arr[7]);
```

```java
        } catch (ArrayIndexOutOfBoundsException e) {
            System.out.println("Array index is out of bounds.");
        }
    }
}
```

SET-5

1. Read and Write to a File:

```java
import java.io.File;
import java.io.FileWriter;
import java.io.FileReader;
import java.io.IOException;

public class FileReadWrite {
    public static void main(String[] args) {
        try {
            File file = new File("test.txt");
            FileWriter writer = new FileWriter(file);
            writer.write("Hello, this is a test.");
            writer.close();

            FileReader reader = new FileReader(file);
            int character;
```

```java
            while ((character = reader.read()) != -1) {
                System.out.print((char) character);
            }
            reader.close();
        } catch (IOException e) {
            System.out.println("An error occurred.");
            e.printStackTrace();
        }
    }
}
```

2. Selection Sort Algorithm:

```java
public class SelectionSort {
    public static void main(String[] args) {
        int[] arr = { 64, 25, 12, 22, 11 };
        for (int i = 0; i < arr.length - 1; i++) {
            int min_idx = i;
            for (int j = i + 1; j < arr.length; j++)
                if (arr[j] < arr[min_idx])
                    min_idx = j;
            int temp = arr[min_idx];
            arr[min_idx] = arr[i];
            arr[i] = temp;
        }
```

```java
        System.out.println("Sorted array: ");
        for (int value : arr) {
            System.out.print(value + " ");
        }
    }
}
```

3. Merge Sort Algorithm:

```java
public class MergeSort {
    void merge(int[] arr, int l, int m, int r) {
        int n1 = m - l + 1;
        int n2 = r - m;
        int[] L = new int[n1];
        int[] R = new int[n2];
        for (int i = 0; i < n1; ++i)
            L[i] = arr[l + i];
        for (int j = 0; j < n2; ++j)
            R[j] = arr[m + 1 + j];
        int i = 0, j = 0;
        int k = l;
        while (i < n1 && j < n2) {
            if (L[i] <= R[j]) {
                arr[k] = L[i];
                i++;
```

```
            } else {
                arr[k] = R[j];
                j++;
            }
            k++;
        }
        while (i < n1) {
            arr[k] = L[i];
            i++;
            k++;
        }
        while (j < n2) {
            arr[k] = R[j];
            j++;
            k++;
        }
    }


    void sort(int[] arr, int l, int r) {
        if (l < r) {
            int m = (l + r) / 2;
            sort(arr, l, m);
            sort(arr, m + 1, r);
            merge(arr, l, m, r);
        }
    }
```

```java
    public static void main(String[] args) {
        int[] arr = { 12, 11, 13, 5, 6, 7 };
        MergeSort ob = new MergeSort();
        ob.sort(arr, 0, arr.length - 1);
        System.out.println("Sorted array:");
        for (int value : arr) {
            System.out.print(value + " ");
        }
    }
}
```

4. Bubble Sort Algorithm:

```java
public class BubbleSort {
    public static void main(String[] args) {
        int[] arr = { 64, 34, 25, 12, 22, 11, 90 };
        int n = arr.length;
        for (int i = 0; i < n - 1; i++)
            for (int j = 0; j < n - i - 1; j++)
                if (arr[j] > arr[j + 1]) {
                    int temp = arr[j];
                    arr[j] = arr[j + 1];
                    arr[j + 1] = temp;
                }
```

```java
        System.out.println("Sorted array: ");
        for (int value : arr) {
            System.out.print(value + " ");
        }
    }
}
```

5. Linear Search Algorithm:

```java
public class LinearSearch {
    public static void main(String[] args) {
        int[] arr = { 2, 3, 4, 10, 40 };
        int target = 10;
        for (int i = 0; i < arr.length; i++) {
            if (arr[i] == target) {
                System.out.println("Element found at index " + i);
                break;
            }
        }
    }
}
```

6. Binary Search Algorithm:

```java
public class BinarySearch {
    int binarySearch(int[] arr, int target) {
        int left = 0, right = arr.length - 1;
        while (left <= right) {
            int mid = left + (right - left) / 2;
            if (arr[mid] == target)
                return mid;
            if (arr[mid] < target)
                left = mid + 1;
            else
                right = mid - 1;
        }
        return -1;
    }

    public static void main(String[] args) {
        BinarySearch bs = new BinarySearch();
        int[] arr = { 2, 3, 4, 10, 40 };
        int target = 10;
        int result = bs.binarySearch(arr, target);
        if (result == -1)
            System.out.println("Element not found");
        else
            System.out.println("Element found at index " + result);
    }
}
```

7. Use of the StringBuilder Class:

```java
public class StringBuilderExample {
    public static void main(String[] args) {
        StringBuilder sb = new StringBuilder("Hello");
        sb.append(" World");
        sb.insert(5, " Java");
        sb.delete(5, 10);
        System.out.println("StringBuilder: " + sb);
    }
}
```

8. Generate Random Numbers:

```java
import java.util.Random;

public class RandomNumber {
    public static void main(String[] args) {
        Random rand = new Random();
        int rand_int1 = rand.nextInt(1000);
        System.out.println("Random Integers: " + rand_int1);
    }
}
```

9. Use of Enum in Java:

```java
enum Day {
    SUNDAY, MONDAY, TUESDAY, WEDNESDAY, THURSDAY, FRIDAY, SATURDAY
}

public class EnumExample {
    public static void main(String[] args) {
        Day day = Day.MONDAY;
        if (day == Day.MONDAY) {
            System.out.println("Yes, it's Monday.");
        } else {
            System.out.println("Not Monday.");
        }
    }
}
```

10. Use of Math Class in Java:

```java
public class MathClassExample {
    public static void main(String[] args) {
        int x = 5;
        int y = 7;
```

```java
        System.out.println

("Maximum of x and y: " + Math.max(x, y));
        System.out.println("Square root of y: " + Math.sqrt(y));
        System.out.println("Power of x and y: " + Math.pow(x, y));
        System.out.println("Logarithm of x: " + Math.log(x));

    }
}
```

SET-6

1. Recursive Fibonacci Series:

```java
public class FibonacciRecursive {
    public static void main(String[] args) {
        int n = 10;
        System.out.print("Fibonacci Series: ");
        for (int i = 0; i < n; i++) {
            System.out.print(fibonacci(i) + " ");
        }
    }

    public static int fibonacci(int n) {
        if (n <= 1)
            return n;
```

```java
        return fibonacci(n - 1) + fibonacci(n - 2);
    }
}
```

2. ArrayList Example:

```java
import java.util.ArrayList;

public class ArrayListExample {
    public static void main(String[] args) {
        ArrayList<String> list = new ArrayList<>();
        list.add("Java");
        list.add("Python");
        list.add("C++");
        list.add("JavaScript");
        System.out.println("Elements in the ArrayList: " + list);
    }
}
```

3. HashSet Example:

```java
import java.util.HashSet;

public class HashSetExample {
```

```java
    public static void main(String[] args) {

        HashSet<String> set = new HashSet<>();

        set.add("Apple");

        set.add("Banana");

        set.add("Orange");

        set.add("Apple"); // Duplicate element

        System.out.println("Elements in the HashSet: " + set);

    }

}
```

4. HashMap Example:

```java
import java.util.HashMap;

public class HashMapExample {

    public static void main(String[] args) {

        HashMap<Integer, String> map = new HashMap<>();

        map.put(1, "John");

        map.put(2, "Doe");

        map.put(3, "Smith");

        System.out.println("Elements in the HashMap: " + map);

    }

}
```

5. Use of the try-catch-finally Block:

```java
public class ExceptionHandling {
    public static void main(String[] args) {
        try {
            int[] arr = new int[5];
            System.out.println(arr[6]);
        } catch (ArrayIndexOutOfBoundsException e) {
            System.out.println("Array index is out of bounds.");
        } finally {
            System.out.println("Finally block is always executed.");
        }
    }
}
```

6. Implement Runnable Interface:

```java
public class RunnableExample {
    public static void main(String[] args) {
        Runnable r = () -> {
            for (int i = 0; i < 5; i++) {
                System.out.println("Child Thread");
            }
        };
        Thread t = new Thread(r);
```

```java
        t.start();

        for (int i = 0; i < 5; i++) {

            System.out.println("Main Thread");

        }

    }

}
```

7. Use of Date and Time in Java:

```java
import java.time.LocalDateTime;

import java.time.format.DateTimeFormatter;


public class DateTimeExample {

    public static void main(String[] args) {

        LocalDateTime currentDateTime = LocalDateTime.now();

        DateTimeFormatter formatter = DateTimeFormatter.ofPattern("yyyy-MM-dd HH:mm:ss");

        String formattedDateTime = currentDateTime.format(formatter);

        System.out.println("Current Date and Time: " + formattedDateTime);

    }

}
```

8. Generate Random Password:

```java
import java.security.SecureRandom;
```

```java
import java.util.Base64;


public class RandomPassword {

    public static void main(String[] args) {

        SecureRandom random = new SecureRandom();

        byte[] bytes = new byte[8];

        random.nextBytes(bytes);

        String password = Base64.getEncoder().encodeToString(bytes);

        System.out.println("Random Password: " + password);

    }

}
```


9. Convert String to Integer:

```java
public class StringToInteger {

    public static void main(String[] args) {

        String str = "12345";

        int number = Integer.parseInt(str);

        System.out.println("Converted integer: " + number);

    }

}
```


10. Generate Random Array:

```java
import java.util.Random;

public class RandomArray {
    public static void main(String[] args) {
        int n = 5;
        int[] arr = new int[n];
        Random random = new Random();
        for (int i = 0; i < n; i++) {
            arr[i] = random.nextInt(50);
        }
        System.out.println("Random Array: ");
        for (int value : arr) {
            System.out.print(value + " ");
        }
    }
}
```

SET-7

1. Thread Example using Thread Class:

```java
class MyThread extends Thread {
    public void run() {
        for (int i = 0; i < 5; i++) {
            System.out.println("Child Thread");
```

```
        }
      }
    }


public class ThreadExample {
    public static void main(String[] args) {
        MyThread t = new MyThread();
        t.start();
        for (int i = 0; i < 5; i++) {
            System.out.println("Main Thread");
        }
    }
}
```

2. Thread Example using Runnable Interface:

```
class MyRunnable implements Runnable {
    public void run() {
        for (int i = 0; i < 5; i++) {
            System.out.println("Child Thread");
        }
    }
}


public class RunnableThreadExample {
```

```java
    public static void main(String[] args) {
        MyRunnable r = new MyRunnable();
        Thread t = new Thread(r);
        t.start();
        for (int i = 0; i < 5; i++) {
            System.out.println("Main Thread");
        }
    }
}
```

3. Read Content from a File:

```java
import java.io.BufferedReader;
import java.io.FileReader;
import java.io.IOException;

public class ReadFile {
    public static void main(String[] args) {
        try {
            BufferedReader reader = new BufferedReader(new FileReader("test.txt"));
            String line;
            while ((line = reader.readLine()) != null) {
                System.out.println(line);
            }
            reader.close();
```

```java
        } catch (IOException e) {
            e.printStackTrace();
        }
    }
}
```

4. Write Content to a File:

```java
import java.io.BufferedWriter;
import java.io.FileWriter;
import java.io.IOException;

public class WriteFile {
    public static void main(String[] args) {
        try {
            BufferedWriter writer = new BufferedWriter(new FileWriter("output.txt"));
            writer.write("Hello, this is a test.");
            writer.close();
            System.out.println("Write successful.");
        } catch (IOException e) {
            e.printStackTrace();
        }
    }
}
```

5. Copy Content from One File to Another:

```java
import java.io.FileReader;
import java.io.FileWriter;
import java.io.IOException;

public class CopyFile {
    public static void main(String[] args) {
        try {
            FileReader reader = new FileReader("input.txt");
            FileWriter writer = new FileWriter("output.txt");
            int character;
            while ((character = reader.read()) != -1) {
                writer.write(character);
            }
            reader.close();
            writer.close();
            System.out.println("Copy successful.");
        } catch (IOException e) {
            e.printStackTrace();
        }
    }
}
```

6. Use of Java Generics:

```java
import java.util.ArrayList;

public class GenericsExample {
    public static void main(String[] args) {
        ArrayList<String> list = new ArrayList<>();
        list.add("Java");
        list.add("Python");
        list.add("C++");
        for (String element : list) {
            System.out.println(element);
        }
    }
}
```

7. Sort an Array using Arrays.sort():

```java
import java.util.Arrays;

public class ArraySorting {
    public static void main(String[] args) {
        int[] arr = { 13, 7, 6, 45, 21, 9, 101, 102 };
        Arrays.sort(arr);
        System.out.println("Sorted Array: " + Arrays.toString(arr));
```

```
        }
    }
```

8. Find the Average of an Array:

```
public class ArrayAverage {
    public static void main(String[] args) {
        int[] numbers = { 2, 4, 6, 8, 10 };
        int sum = 0;
        for (int number : numbers) {
            sum += number;
        }
        double average = (double) sum / numbers.length;
        System.out.println("Average of the array: " + average);
    }
}
```

9. Use of Lambda Expressions in Java:

```
interface MyInterface {
    void display();
}

public class LambdaExample {
```

```java
    public static void main(String[] args) {
        MyInterface obj = () -> System.out.println("Hello from Lambda");
        obj.display();
    }
}
```

10. Use of Command Line Arguments:

```java
public class CommandLineArguments {
    public static void main(String[] args) {
        if (args.length > 0) {
            System.out.println("The command line arguments are: ");
            for (String arg : args) {
                System.out.println(arg);
            }
        } else {
            System.out.println("No command line arguments found.");
        }
    }
}
```

SET-8

1. Create a Server-Side Socket:

```java
import java.io.*;
import java.net.*;

public class ServerSocketExample {
    public static void main(String[] args) {
        try {
            ServerSocket serverSocket = new ServerSocket(8080);
            Socket socket = serverSocket.accept();
            System.out.println("Server connected to " + socket.getInetAddress());
            serverSocket.close();
        } catch (IOException e) {
            e.printStackTrace();
        }
    }
}
```

2. Create a Client-Side Socket:

```java
import java.io.*;
import java.net.*;

public class ClientSocketExample {
    public static void main(String[] args) {
```

```java
        try {
            Socket socket = new Socket("localhost", 8080);
            System.out.println("Client connected to the server.");
            socket.close();
        } catch (IOException e) {
            e.printStackTrace();
        }
    }
}
```

3. Use of Regular Expressions in Java:

```java
import java.util.regex.Matcher;
import java.util.regex.Pattern;

public class RegexExample {
    public static void main(String[] args) {
        String content = "The quick brown fox jumps over the lazy dog";
        String patternString = ".*fox.*";
        Pattern pattern = Pattern.compile(patternString);
        Matcher matcher = pattern.matcher(content);
        if (matcher.matches()) {
            System.out.println("Pattern found in the content.");
        } else {
            System.out.println("Pattern not found in the content.");
```

```
        }
    }
}
```

4. Read Input from Console:

```java
import java.util.Scanner;

public class ReadInputFromConsole {
    public static void main(String[] args) {
        Scanner scanner = new Scanner(System.in);
        System.out.print("Enter your name: ");
        String name = scanner.nextLine();
        System.out.println("Hello, " + name);
        scanner.close();
    }
}
```

5. Write Output to Console:

```java
public class WriteOutputToConsole {
    public static void main(String[] args) {
        System.out.println("Hello, World!");
    }
```

```
}
```

6. Use of Polymorphism in Java:

```java
class Animal {
    void sound() {
        System.out.println("Animal is making a sound.");
    }
}

class Dog extends Animal {
    void sound() {
        System.out.println("Dog is barking.");
    }
}

class Cat extends Animal {
    void sound() {
        System.out.println("Cat is meowing.");
    }
}

public class PolymorphismExample {
    public static void main(String[] args) {
        Animal animal1 = new Dog();
```

```java
        Animal animal2 = new Cat();

        animal1.sound();

        animal2.sound();

    }

}
```

7. Find the Minimum and Maximum Element in an Array:

```java
import java.util.Arrays;

public class MinMaxArray {
    public static void main(String[] args) {
        int[] arr = { 10, 4, 7, 5, 2, 8 };
        Arrays.sort(arr);
        System.out.println("Minimum element: " + arr[0]);
        System.out.println("Maximum element: " + arr[arr.length - 1]);
    }
}
```

8. Use of String Formatting in Java:

```java
public class StringFormatting {
    public static void main(String[] args) {
        String name = "John";
```

```java
        int age = 30;

        double salary = 50000.50;

        System.out.printf("Name: %s, Age: %d, Salary: %.2f", name, age, salary);

    }

}
```

9. Check if a Number is Positive or Negative:

```java
import java.util.Scanner;

public class PositiveNegativeCheck {
    public static void main(String[] args) {
        Scanner scanner = new Scanner(System.in);
        System.out.print("Enter a number: ");
        int number = scanner.nextInt();
        if (number > 0) {
            System.out.println("The number is positive.");
        } else if (number < 0) {
            System.out.println("The number is negative.");
        } else {
            System.out.println("The number is zero.");
        }
        scanner.close();
    }
}
```

10. Reverse a String:

```java
public class ReverseString {
    public static void main(String[] args) {
        String str = "Hello, World!";
        StringBuilder sb = new StringBuilder(str);
        sb.reverse();
        System.out.println("Reversed string: " + sb);
    }
}
```

SET-9

1. Implement a Stack Data Structure:

```java
import java.util.Stack;

public class StackExample {
    public static void main(String[] args) {
        Stack<Integer> stack = new Stack<>();
        stack.push(1);
        stack.push(2);
        stack.push(3);
```

```java
        System.out.println("Elements in the stack: " + stack);

        System.out.println("Popped element: " + stack.pop());

        System.out.println("Top element: " + stack.peek());

    }

}
```

2. Implement a Queue Data Structure:

```java
import java.util.LinkedList;

import java.util.Queue;

public class QueueExample {

    public static void main(String[] args) {

        Queue<String> queue = new LinkedList<>();

        queue.add("A");

        queue.add("B");

        queue.add("C");

        System.out.println("Elements in the queue: " + queue);

        System.out.println("Removed element: " + queue.remove());

        System.out.println("Head of the queue: " + queue.peek());

    }

}
```

3. Binary Search Algorithm:

```java
public class BinarySearchExample {
    public static int binarySearch(int[] arr, int target) {
        int left = 0, right = arr.length - 1;
        while (left <= right) {
            int mid = left + (right - left) / 2;
            if (arr[mid] == target)
                return mid;
            if (arr[mid] < target)
                left = mid + 1;
            else
                right = mid - 1;
        }
        return -1;
    }

    public static void main(String[] args) {
        int[] arr = { 2, 3, 4, 10, 40 };
        int target = 10;
        int result = binarySearch(arr, target);
        if (result == -1)
            System.out.println("Element not found");
        else
            System.out.println("Element found at index " + result);
    }
}
```

4. Depth-First Search (DFS) Algorithm:

```java
import java.util.ArrayList;
import java.util.List;

class Graph {
    private int V;
    private List<List<Integer>> adj;

    Graph(int v) {
        V = v;
        adj = new ArrayList<>(v);
        for (int i = 0; i < v; ++i)
            adj.add(new ArrayList<>());
    }

    void addEdge(int v, int w) {
        adj.get(v).add(w);
    }

    void DFSUtil(int v, boolean[] visited) {
        visited[v] = true;
        System.out.print(v + " ");
        for (Integer n : adj.get(v)) {
```

```java
        if (!visited[n])
            DFSUtil(n, visited);
    }
}

void DFS(int v) {
    boolean[] visited = new boolean[V];
    DFSUtil(v, visited);
}

public static void main(String[] args) {
    Graph g = new Graph(4);
    g.addEdge(0, 1);
    g.addEdge(0, 2);
    g.addEdge(1, 2);
    g.addEdge(2, 0);
    g.addEdge(2, 3);
    g.addEdge(3, 3);
    System.out.println("Following is Depth First Traversal " + "(starting from vertex 2)");
    g.DFS(2);
}
}
```

5. Breadth-First Search (BFS) Algorithm:

```java
import java.util.Iterator;
import java.util.LinkedList;

class GraphBFS {
    private int V;
    private LinkedList<Integer> adj[];

    GraphBFS(int v) {
        V = v;
        adj = new LinkedList[v];
        for (int i = 0; i < v; ++i)
            adj[i] = new LinkedList();
    }

    void addEdge(int v, int w) {
        adj[v].add(w);
    }

    void BFS(int s) {
        boolean visited[] = new boolean[V];
        LinkedList<Integer> queue = new LinkedList<>();
        visited[s] = true;
        queue.add(s);
        while (queue.size() != 0) {
            s = queue.poll();
            System.out.print(s + " ");
```

```java
        Iterator<Integer> i = adj[s].listIterator();
        while (i.hasNext()) {
            int n = i.next();
            if (!visited[n]) {
                visited[n] = true;
                queue.add(n);
            }
        }
    }
}

public static void main(String[] args) {
    GraphBFS g = new GraphBFS(4);
    g.addEdge(0, 1);
    g.addEdge(0, 2);
    g.addEdge(1, 2);
    g.addEdge(2, 0);
    g.addEdge(2, 3);
    g.addEdge(3, 3);
    System.out.println("Following is Breadth First Traversal " + "(starting from vertex 2)");
    g.BFS(2);
}
}
```

6. Use of StringBuilder for String Manipulation:

```java
public class StringBuilderExample {
    public static void main(String[] args) {
        StringBuilder sb = new StringBuilder();
        sb.append("Java");
        sb.append(" is");
        sb.append(" awesome");
        System.out.println("Result: " + sb.toString());
    }
}
```

7. Convert a String to Uppercase:

```java
public class StringToUppercase {
    public static void main(String[] args) {
        String str = "hello world";
        String strUpper = str.toUpperCase();
        System.out.println("Uppercase string: " + strUpper);
    }
}
```

8. Convert a String to Lowercase:

```java
public class StringToLowercase {
```

```java
    public static void main(String[] args) {
        String str = "HELLO WORLD";
        String strLower =

 str.toLowerCase();
        System.out.println("Lowercase string: " + strLower);
    }
}
```

9. Use of the Math.random() Method:

```java
public class RandomNumberExample {
    public static void main(String[] args) {
        double rand = Math.random();
        System.out.println("Random number between 0 and 1: " + rand);
    }
}
```

10. Use of the Math.abs() Method:

```java
public class AbsoluteValueExample {
    public static void main(String[] args) {
        int num = -10;
        int absNum = Math.abs(num);
```

```java
        System.out.println("Absolute value of " + num + " is " + absNum);
    }
}
```

SET-10

1. Use of Synchronized Method:

```java
class Table {
    synchronized void printTable(int n) {
        for (int i = 1; i <= 5; i++) {
            System.out.println(n * i);
            try {
                Thread.sleep(400);
            } catch (InterruptedException e) {
                System.out.println(e);
            }
        }
    }
}

class MyThread1 extends Thread {
    Table t;

    MyThread1(Table t) {
```

```java
            this.t = t;
        }

        public void run() {
            t.printTable(5);
        }
    }

    class MyThread2 extends Thread {
        Table t;

        MyThread2(Table t) {
            this.t = t;
        }

        public void run() {
            t.printTable(100);
        }
    }

    public class SynchronizedExample {
        public static void main(String[] args) {
            Table obj = new Table();
            MyThread1 t1 = new MyThread1(obj);
            MyThread2 t2 = new MyThread2(obj);
            t1.start();
```

```
        t2.start();
    }
}
```

2. Use of Try-Catch Blocks for Exception Handling:

```
public class ExceptionHandlingExample {
    public static void main(String[] args) {
        try {
            int data = 50 / 0; // may throw exception
        } catch (ArithmeticException e) {
            System.out.println(e);
        }
        System.out.println("rest of the code");
    }
}
```

3. Use of Multiple Catch Blocks:

```
public class MultipleCatchExample {
    public static void main(String[] args) {
        try {
            int a[] = new int[5];
            a[5] = 30 / 0;
```

```java
        } catch (ArithmeticException e) {

            System.out.println("Arithmetic Exception occurs");

        } catch (ArrayIndexOutOfBoundsException e) {

            System.out.println("ArrayIndexOutOfBounds Exception occurs");

        } catch (Exception e) {

            System.out.println("Parent Exception occurs");

        }

        System.out.println("rest of the code");

    }

}
```

4. Use of Finally Block:

```java
public class FinallyExample {

    public static void main(String[] args) {

        try {

            int data = 25 / 5;

            System.out.println(data);

        } catch (NullPointerException e) {

            System.out.println(e);

        } finally {

            System.out.println("finally block is always executed");

        }

        System.out.println("rest of the code");

    }
```

```
}
```

5. Use of Throw Keyword:

```java
public class ThrowExample {
    static void checkAge(int age) {
        if (age < 18)
            throw new ArithmeticException("Not Eligible to Vote");
        else
            System.out.println("Eligible to Vote");
    }

    public static void main(String[] args) {
        checkAge(15);
        System.out.println("rest of the code");
    }
}
```

6. Use of Custom Exception:

```java
class MyException extends Exception {
    MyException(String s) {
        super(s);
    }
```

```java
}

public class CustomExceptionExample {
    public static void main(String[] args) {
        try {
            throw new MyException("This is my custom exception");
        } catch (MyException e) {
            System.out.println(e);
        }
    }
}
```

7. Implement Runnable Interface with Thread:

```java
public class RunnableThreadExample {
    public static void main(String[] args) {
        Runnable r = () -> {
            for (int i = 0; i < 5; i++) {
                System.out.println("Child Thread");
            }
        };
        Thread t = new Thread(r);
        t.start();
        for (int i = 0; i < 5; i++) {
            System.out.println("Main Thread");
```

```
        }

    }

}
```

8. Use of Nested Class in Java:

```java
public class Outer {

    private int data = 30;

    class Inner {

        void display() {

            System.out.println("data is " + data);

        }

    }

    public static void main(String args[]) {

        Outer obj = new Outer();

        Outer.Inner in = obj.new Inner();

        in.display();

    }

}
```

9. Use of Anonymous Class in Java:

```java
abstract class Anonymous {

    abstract void display();

}


public class AnonymousClassExample {

    public static void main(String[] args) {

        Anonymous obj = new Anonymous() {

            void display() {

                System.out.println("Anonymous Class Example");

            }

        };

        obj.display();

    }

}
```

10. Use of Interface in Java:

```java
interface Drawable {

    void draw();

}


class Rectangle implements Drawable {

    public void draw() {

        System.out.println("drawing rectangle");

    }
```

```java
    }


class Circle implements Drawable {
    public void draw() {
        System.out.println("drawing circle");
    }
}


public class InterfaceExample {
    public static void main(String[] args) {
        Drawable d = new Circle();
        d.draw();
    }
}
```